Which Native Tree?

A Simple Guide to the Identification of New Zealand Native Trees

Andrew Crowe

PENGUIN BOOKS

About the Author

Andrew Crowe is a full-time natural history writer with a special interest in New Zealand native trees and their uses. His books include *A Field Guide to the Native Edible Plants of New Zealand* (1981), *The Which Plant Poster Series* (1991) and several wildlife books for children. He has compiled *Which Native Tree?* in response to popular demand for a simple method of identifying New Zealand native trees.

Acknowledgements

Thanks to Rae West (*A Guide to Trees*) and Alan Esler (*Common Trees and Shrubs of the Waitakere Range*) for the basic idea of a key based on leaves.

Many people offered valuable comments; in particular, I would like to thank Alan Esler, John Smith-Dodsworth, Ewen Cameron and Fred Overmars. For help with some of the details on insects, my thanks to Olwyn and Chris Green.

A list of those friends and colleagues who sustained me with their advice, criticism, support and enthusiasm would indeed be long, but a special thank you to Claire Paterson.

Details on the many plant uses came from a wide range of conversations, specialist books and papers – too many to list here. Deserving special acknowledgement, however, are those Māori elders of the 19th and early 20th centuries who, though part of a culture where knowledge is traditionally guarded as a source of power, chose to share that knowledge rather than risk its being lost forever.

Finally, my thanks to everyone who has ever moved in defence of our wild places; without you there would be little to write about.

Andrew Crowe

PENGUIN BOOKS

Penguin Books (NZ) Ltd, cnr Rosedale and Airborne Roads, Albany, Auckland 1310, New Zealand
Penguin Books Ltd, 27 Wrights Lane, London W8 5TZ, England
Penguin USA, 375 Hudson Street, New York, NY 10014, United States
Penguin Books Australia Ltd, 487 Maroondah Highway, Ringwood, Australia 3134
Penguin Books Canada Ltd, 10 Alcorn Avenue, Toronto, Ontario, Canada M4V 3B2
Penguin Books (South Africa) Pty Ltd, 4 Pallinghurst Road, Parktown, Johannesburg 2193, South Africa

Penguin Books Ltd, Registered Offices: Harmondsworth, Middlesex, England

First published by Penguin Books (NZ) Ltd, 1992
Reprinted 1992 (two times), 1993, 1994 (two times), 1996, 1998
This edition published 1999, reprinted 2000, 2001

10 9 8 7 6 5 4 3

Designed by Jan Maxim
Edited by Brian O'Flaherty
Illustrations: Geoffrey Cox
Photographs: Andrew Crowe
Design concept: Andrew Crowe

Printed by South Wind Production (Singapore) Pte Ltd

Using this Book

Almost all New Zealand native trees are evergreen, so the simplest way to identify them is by their leaves. Rather than having to flick randomly through hundreds of illustrations, this book provides instead a very simple leaf key.

Before using the leaf keys

To be precise, trees have either 'simple' leaves or 'compound' ones made up of individual 'leaflets'. But the layperson (and this book) generally refers to both leaves and leaflets simply as 'leaves'.*

Basically, there are three ways in which leaves (or leaflets) are arranged on a branch or stalk: hand-shaped, alternating, or opposite.

Hand-shaped (with three or more fingers) **Alternating** **Opposite** (all in pairs)

Some leaves have teeth along the edges, others have none.

Teeth **No teeth**

When measuring the length, don't include the leaf stalk. A leaf is narrow if its length is more than twice the width. A leaf is broad if its length is less than twice the width.

Length **Narrow** **Broad**

Using the leaf keys

1 Find a typical leaf of a common, adult, native tree. Don't pull it off because later you'll need to look at how it grows on the tree. Now turn to page 5 and decide which type of leaf it is. (Start at the bottom of the chart.) Then turn to the page indicated.

2 Starting from the arrow at the bottom of this new page, follow the appropriate branches until you arrive at an illustration of your leaf. Now turn to the page indicated for a close-up photograph of that leaf.

3 Just to be sure, run down the checklist next to the photograph.

If you have any trouble matching your leaf to the key or run into any problems (like not being able to reach the leaves), turn to *Troubleshooting* on page 62.

---

*Later, as you get to know more about trees, it will help to know the difference between a simple leaf and a group of leaflets that makes up a compound leaf. Leaf buds are the clue. If it has a bud at its base, then it is a leaf and not a leaflet. (Examples of compound leaves in this book are kohekohe, tītoki, kōwhai, patē, whauwhaupaku and pūriri.)

Using the tree pages

Trees that share similar characteristics appear on facing pages. Use the identification checklists on these pages to distinguish between them. The following graphics show the usual distribution and common size for each tree.

A guide to the latitudinal limits within which the wild tree is usually found.

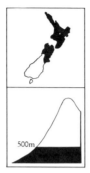

The common shape and height of the mature tree with an adult person to give scale.

12m

A guide to the altitudes where the tree naturally grows (in metres).

500m

Another approach: the flowers and berries key

If the tree has large, conspicuous flowers or fruits, there is a more direct approach: turn to page 61. What colour is the flower or fruit? Follow that coloured band up the diagram until you arrive at the appropriate flower or fruit. Turn to the page indicated and use the checklist on that page.

Māori names

Many Māori plant names are regional. Although it is necessary in a book like this to keep to the names most widely used, local variations are just as valid. The correct pronunciation of Māori vowels is as follows: *a* as in *far*, *e* as in b*e*t, *i* as in m*e*, *o* as in *awe*, *u* as in m*oo*n. To help with pronunciation, the macrons have been included; these indicate a lengthened vowel, e.g. ā=aa.

Tree uses

It is my hope that learning the uses of trees will foster your appreciation of them, but it could lead to thoughtless damage too. For example, taking bark from a living tree for, say, wool dyeing can easily kill that tree. As a general rule it would be hard to beat the maxim displayed in many publicly owned forests:

Take only photographs;
leave only footprints.

It would, of course, be hypocritical if this did not apply equally to companies wishing to mill and mine our dwindling wilderness.

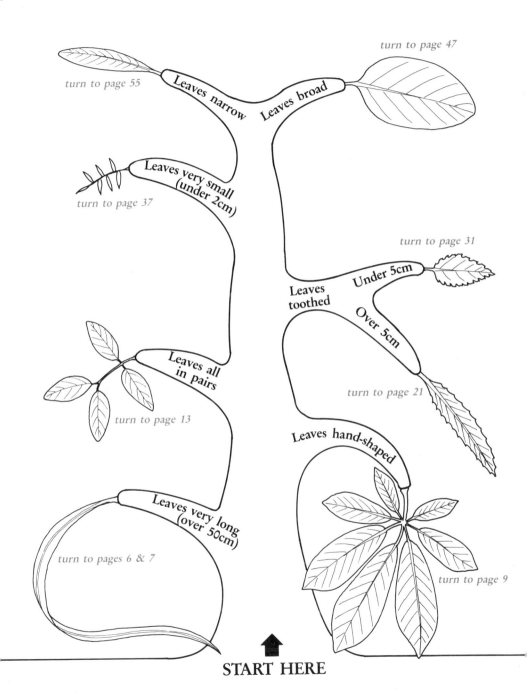

turn to page 47

turn to page 55

Leaves narrow

Leaves broad

Leaves very small
(under 2cm)

turn to page 37

turn to page 31

Leaves
toothed

Under 5cm

Over 5cm

Leaves all
in pairs

turn to page 13

turn to page 21

Leaves hand-shaped

Leaves very long
(over 50cm)

turn to pages 6 & 7

turn to page 9

START HERE

Tī Kōuka
Cabbage Tree
Cordyline australis

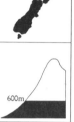

12m

Leaves: 50cm–1m long, narrow, *grass-like*, growing in tufts

Flowers: in late spring, white, sweetly scented

Fruit: in late summer, small, bluish-white

Trunk: *spongy to touch*, like cork

Other: common in swamps and flood plains

Nature Notes: fruit popular with bellbird and wood pigeon. Bees collect the nectar. On the undersides of dead leaves, look for the remarkably well-camouflaged cabbage tree moth (wingspan 4cm).

Uses: The roots and stems are so rich in sugar that tests were carried out in the mid-1980s to see if the tree might be grown commercially. Though high in fructose, as an economic food crop it may not be viable. The cooked tap roots, the core of the trunk and the tender shoots were, however, all important foods of early Māori.

The leaves of the various types of cabbage tree provided a source of fibre for weaving baskets, making bird snares, rope and string, rain capes, sandals and thatching. They were also brewed into a tea used to cure dysentery and diarrhoea, and scrapings from leaves were applied to cuts and sores. New shoots were reportedly boiled and eaten by nursing mothers and colicky children. Rural children continue to enjoy using the branches, complete with their leaf heads, as makeshift sledges for grassy slopes. In the 1860s, at one of England's largest papermills, paper made from the leaves received high praise, but high cartage costs thwarted a commercial venture.

Planted for subtropical effect, especially as a small group, or even as a tub plant, cabbage trees are best placed away from lawns and buildings to prevent their falling leaves becoming a nuisance. Grows easily and quickly from seed but beware of pūkeko pulling out young plants to eat their roots. Can also be grown from cuttings. At least five cultivated forms are available.

Nīkau
Rhopalostylis sapida

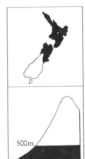

Leaves: typical *palm fronds*, meet to form a bulbous head

Flowers: late spring to early autumn, small, pink, hang in long spreading fingers

Fruit: mostly in late summer/ early autumn, small, red, in finger-like bunches

Trunk: usually unbranched, with circular leaf scars

Nature Notes: fruit eaten mainly by wood pigeon and sometimes kākā and kākāriki. Seeds used occasionally as gizzard stones by kiwi. Bees collect the nectar.

Uses: The fronds provided Māori with an effective roofing material and the leaf strips were woven into kete and other baskets, while the rounded base of the fallen frond made a useful bowl-like container. Later, these fronds were used by rural children to make sledges for grassy slopes.

The ripe, red fruit may look edible but consists mostly of hard seed, so hard that they were once used by settlers for bird shooting when other forms of ammunition were scarce. The undeveloped leaves that form the heart of the nīkau tree do, however, provide a valuable emergency food but its removal kills the palm. Nevertheless it was an occasional Māori food, eaten raw or cooked and sometimes taken medicinally to ease childbirth. Likewise, the pink immature flowers, while still enclosed in their green sheaths, are edible but fortunately with less cost to the tree.

If short of water, it is possible in an emergency to slit a hole in the base of the bulbous swelling at the top of the trunk to allow collected rainwater to drain out.

A very attractive and distinctively tropical landscaping tree, especially when planted as a grove, but sensitive to wind and withstands only light frosts. Grown from seed – cover first with boiling water to soften the coating. Slow to germinate.

Pūriri
Vitex lucens

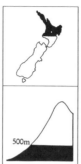

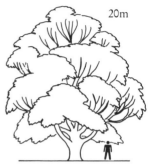

20m

500m

Leaves: hand-shaped, with 3–5 'fingers', *no teeth* (unlike whauwhaupaku), glossy, bulging between veins, leaf stalks square-angled

Flowers: throughout year, but particularly in winter, pinkish-red, 2.5cm long

Fruit: throughout year, round, red, 2cm across

Nature Notes: fruit is popular with wood pigeon, tui and kākā; the nectar with bellbird, tui and silvereye. Bees concentrate more on the pollen. Holes in the trunk are often made by the pūriri moth caterpillar.

Uses: Māori have used infusions of pūriri leaves for bathing muscular aches and sprains, and as a remedy for ulcers and sore throats. Today, a patented germicide is derived from a compound found in the leaves.

It provided early Māori with a source of yellow dye for colouring flax weaving. As with most plant dyes, this was made from the bark, though it should be emphasised that bark stripping can easily destroy a living tree. Plant dye enthusiasts have continued the tradition, using either pūriri bark or sawdust to produce maize yellow with an alum or chrome mordant, or the ripe berries with an alum and soda mordant for primrose yellow.

The wood is said to be New Zealand's strongest and most durable and was therefore used for piles, fenceposts, railway sleepers, bridges, etc. It is so difficult to split that timberworkers often resorted to dynamite. Though its swirling grain makes it a hard wood to work, it is still valued for woodturning and some furniture.

A useful shade or specimen tree. Attracts birds. Grows easily from seed – cover first with boiling water and soak overnight to soften the coating. Can also be grown from side cuttings taken low down on the tree; include a chip of bark for best results.

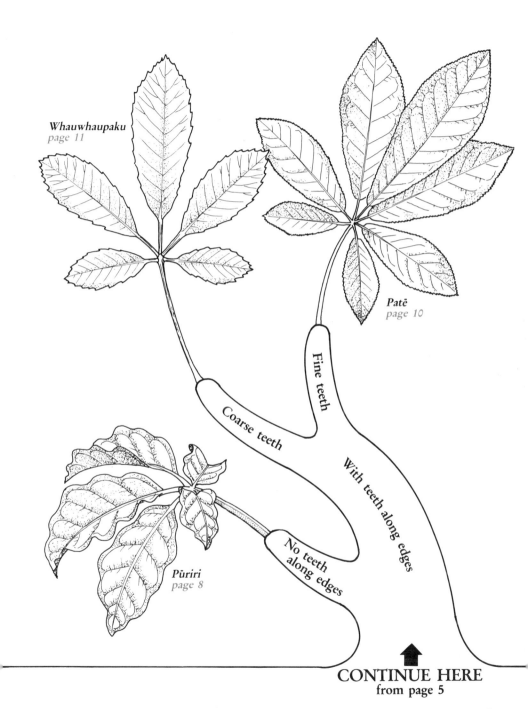

Whauwhaupaku
page 11

Patē
page 10

Fine teeth

Coarse teeth

With teeth along edges

Pūriri
page 8

No teeth
along edges

CONTINUE HERE
from page 5

Patē
Seven Finger

Schefflera digitata

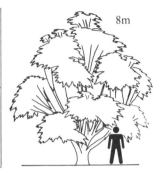

8m

1200m

Leaves: hand-shaped, with 7–9 'fingers', *fine* teeth, *thin, limp* (unlike whauwhaupaku)

Flowers: late summer, small, greenish, *hang in long fingers* (unlike whauwhaupaku)

Fruit: in autumn (female trees only), very small, purple-black, in long fingers

Other: found mainly along the edges of forest

Nature Notes: fruit attractive to birds, such as silvereye, tui and bellbird.

Uses: Māori used the sap to heal ringworm and sores caused by tuberculosis of the lymph glands. The leaves have since been shown to contain falcarindiol which has the specific effect of inhibiting germination of the spores of common skin fungi, such as those that cause ringworm. Newborn babies were also wrapped in patē leaves (along with those of the large-leaved coprosma and hen and chickens fern) until they perspired.

The softness of the wood made patē well suited for use with kaikōmako for the Māori method of creating fire: a pointed stick of kaikōmako was scraped up and down a patē slab until the accumulating patē dust caught alight by friction (see kaikōmako for details).

The ripe, dark purple berries have been used (with an alum mordant) for dyeing wool wine coloured, grey-blue (with alum and soda), mauve (with cream of tartar and tin), or green (with a bichromate of potash mordant).

Patē is recommended for planting to attract birds, and in British sun lounges it has become a lasting favourite for its tropical appearance. Grows best here in reasonable soil with some shade and is propagated either by seed or from cuttings. In the North Island, the leaves of seedlings are often attractively lobed like long oak leaves.

Whauwhaupaku
Five Finger
Pseudopanax arboreus

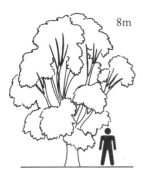

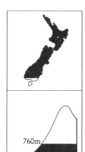

Leaves: hand-shaped, with 5–7 'fingers', *large teeth, thick and leathery* (unlike patē)

Flowers: in winter, tiny, sweet scented, in ball-like clusters

Fruit: in spring (female trees only), tiny, black, in ball-like clusters

Other: the more southern orihou (mountain five finger) usually has no stalks on its 'fingers'

Nature Notes: hairy, green caterpillars of the five finger plume moth often chew leaves. Silvereye and tui eat the fruit. Possums chew off leaf stalks. Bees relish nectar.

Names: Here is an excellent example of a tree whose name varies among regions. Though called puahou in the Bay of Plenty area, its most common Māori name is whauwhaupaku. And what to many is five finger was once known in Taranaki as 'snotty gob', presumably for the clear, tasteless, glue-like substance often found on the growing bud.

Uses: To Tūhoe Māori its fruiting marked the fourth month of their calendar (September). The bark was sometimes used to make small water-carrying containers. The ripe berries, while quite inedible (extremely bitter), do make reasonably good wool dyes: purple, khaki, yellow-green, yellow-brown and grey using an alum mordant; mauve, purple or wine with cream of tartar and tin; grey-green with alum and iron; sage green with alum and copper; reseda green if a bichromate of potash mordant is used.

Makes a pretty specimen tree or shrubbery plant and will grow in tubs or pots. Very hardy, withstands wind, but looks best when well fed to produce larger leaves. Has strikingly geometrical flowers and fruit, and flowers have a sweet, honey scent. Grows easily from fresh, ripe seed or semi-hardwood cuttings, i.e. partially matured or ripened wood taken after a new flush of growth. Good for attracting birds.

Kawakawa

Macropiper excelsum

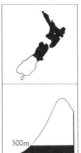

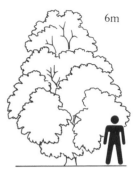

6m

Leaves: opposite each other, *heart-shaped* (unlike most native trees), *spicy smell* when crushed, usually full of holes

Fruit: mostly in summer (female trees only), yellow-orange, usually 2–5cm long

Other: purplish-brown branches, *jointed like crooked bamboo*

Nature Notes: fruit popular with wood pigeon. Brown looper caterpillars (up to 3cm long) commonly eat holes in the leaves and can often be seen on the undersides.

Uses: To kill insects that injured their kūmara plants, Māori gardeners set fire to wet, green kawakawa leaves and branches laid in rows between their plantation beds. As the kawakawa smouldered, its acrid smoke poisoned the pests. The leaves and branches have since been found to contain a compound that can kill insects by interfering with their metamorphoses. (The large, brown looper caterpillar so common on kawakawa leaves has a peculiar immunity to this.)

The list of kawakawa's medicinal uses is long, but one such use – that of chewing the leaves to alleviate toothache – has a sound chemical basis. Kawakawa contains myristicin, a substance similar to the pain-numbing constituent of cloves.

The ripe, orange fruit was eaten raw (after spitting out the tiny, spicy, black seeds) and even used to flavour a kind of jelly made from seaweed. The leaves are sometimes made into tea. Spinners have found that the branches and leaves will dye wool lime green with a chrome mordant, bluish-green with copper.

Attracts birds, is tolerant of shade or sun and the occasional pruning, has an attractive compact shape and can be grown in a tub or pot. Grows easily from either seed or cuttings. Does best when sheltered from frost.

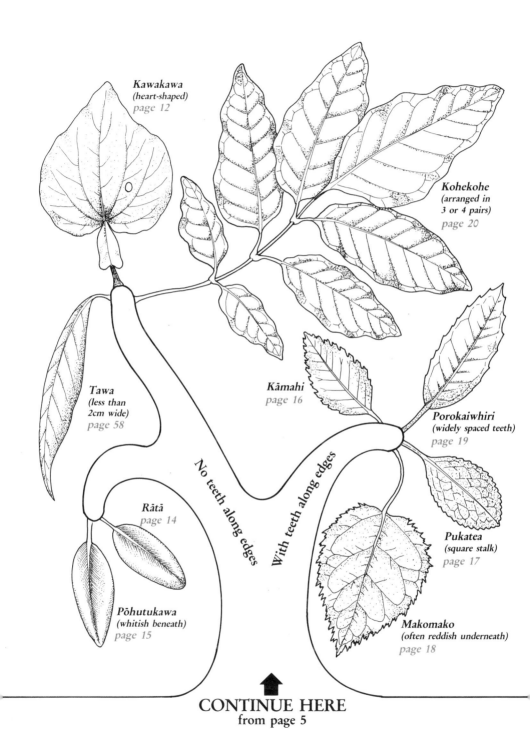

Kawakawa
(heart-shaped)
page 12

Kohekohe
(arranged in
3 or 4 pairs)
page 20

Tawa
(less than
2cm wide)
page 58

Kāmahi
page 16

Porokaiwhiri
(widely spaced teeth)
page 19

No teeth along edges

With teeth along edges

Rātā
page 14

Pukatea
(square stalk)
page 17

Pōhutukawa
(whitish beneath)
page 15

Makomako
(often reddish underneath)
page 18

CONTINUE HERE
from page 5

13

Rātā
(Northern) *Metrosideros robusta*
(Southern) *Metrosideros umbellata*

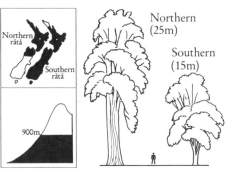

Leaves: opposite each other, *green underneath* (unlike pōhutukawa), leaf tips on northern rātā indented and rounder than southern rātā

Flowers: in summer, red, in spiky balls

Other: northern rātā often starts life as a vine, later engulfing its host

Nature Notes: flax-like astelias, kahakaha and kiekie are common in the branches. Bellbird, tui, kākā, kea and bees eat the nectar. Young leaves a favourite of the possum.

Differences: Southern rātā is a medium-sized tree, starting life as a seed in the ground. Northern rātā, however, often begins life high up in the forks of other trees, later sending roots down to engulf its dead or dying host.

Uses: Known uses refer mostly to the northern rātā, but southern rātā can often be used in the same way. The nectar from its striking red flowers was used by early Māori both as a food and as a remedy for sore throats. Interestingly, these flowers have since been shown to contain known antiseptics such as gallic acid. As a remedy for diarrhoea, an infusion of the inner bark was used; the bark has since been found to contain ellagic acid – an effective astringent for diarrhoea and dysentery. The outer bark has a variety of medicinal uses too, and later was recommended to tanners for its high tannin content. Homespinners use it with various mordants to produce 'good' fawn and light brown dyes.

As a timber, its hardness, strength and durability made it suitable for everything from machine bearings, shipbuilding and bridge construction to cartwheels. It is still regarded as ideal for mallet heads and carving-chisel handles, and is recommended for furniture and woodturning.

Both types of rātā can be grown as garden plants but have the disadvantage of taking many years to produce flowers.

Pōhutukawa
Metrosideros excelsa

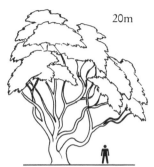

20m

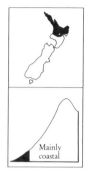

Mainly coastal

Leaves: opposite each other (unlike karo), *velvety white underneath* (unlike rātā), usually 5–8cm long
Flowers: in early summer, red, in large spiky balls
Trunk: gnarled and spreading
Other: most noticeable on coastal cliffs, has *white branchlets*

Nature Notes: flowers are an important source of nectar for bees, bellbird and tui. Young growth a favourite of the possum, which threatens its survival in the wild.

Uses: Also known as the New Zealand Christmas tree for the timing of its flowering, this is certainly one of our most beautiful and spectacular trees.

An infusion of its inner bark was used to cure dysentery and diarrhoea – not surprising since pōhutukawa contains ellagic acid, an astringent used for both ailments. Māori also collected its nectar for food and to treat sore throats; it was said to have been sucked out through a reed, though you can just poke your tongue into the flower as the tui and bellbird do.

The deep red timber is extremely strong and durable, used from the earliest time of European settlement for making stems and knees in boatbuilding. A dense, hard-wearing wood, it was used in bearings and machine beds, framing and sills of dock gates and the like. It makes good firewood too.

Though growing naturally only in northern regions, it is widely planted (mostly as a coastal tree) as far south as Dunedin. A great specimen tree, it can also be used for hedging or shelter. Grows easily from fresh seed (collected in February or March) but semi-hardwood cuttings have the advantage of bypassing the tender juvenile stage and flowering much sooner. To collect the tiny, dust-like seed, hold a bag over a cluster of seed capsules and shake. Sow thinly.

Kāmahi

Weinmannia racemosa

25m

900m

Leaves: opposite (unlike beech), 3–10cm long (smaller and less leathery on juveniles), large teeth

Flowers: late spring/early summer, almost white, fluffy, in finger-like clusters

Other: north of Auckland a slightly smaller-leaved form is found, called tōwai.

Nature Notes: bees collect nectar and pollen between November and January. Leaves a favourite of the possum.

Uses: In Māori medicine, inner kāmahi bark was steeped in hot water and the liquid drunk as a laxative; the bark itself (which contains astringent tannins and catechin) was similarly infused to make a tonic.

This same bark yielded a black dye used by Māori on cabbage tree and flax leaves. With more modern mordants, homespinners have produced yellow-fawn (with alum), a brighter yellow-fawn (with alum and soda) and a deep yellow-fawn (with copper).

Kāmahi provided 19th century leather tanners with one of their primary raw materials. The air-dried bark of young trees contains over 8% tannin (and older trees double this), making it one of the richest native sources of tannin. It was used extensively in several Auckland tanneries and for a few years during the 19th century was even exported.

As a timber, kāmahi was not only put to many below-ground uses (piles, fenceposts, sleepers, etc) but its figured wood was, and still is, used by woodturners. With cabinetmakers it has been less popular: it tends to warp badly and the large diameter logs needed for milling boards are too often hollow.

In the garden or park, it is the flowers and occasionally-red winter leaves that make it worth planting. Indeed, the foliage has often been used in formal flower arranging. Most often grown from seed but can be grown from cuttings.

Pukatea
Laurelia novae-zelandiae

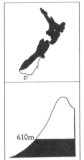

35m

610m

Leaves: *opposite* (unlike beech), round even teeth, *stalks square-angled* (unlike kāmahi), dark glossy green, veins inconspicuous

Fruit: late summer, seed cases green, jug-shaped, releasing fluffy seeds in autumn

Trunk: distinct plank-like buttresses at base

Other: prefers damp places

Nature Notes: bees collect white pollen from the inconspicuous yellow-green flowers in October and November.

Uses: Medicinally, pukatea's inner bark was boiled or pulped by early Māori and used internally for the relief of ulcers, skin complaints and toothache, and both internally and externally for syphilis; its fresh bark steeped in hot water for neuralgia. Its painkilling properties have since been proven by chemists: the leaves act as both a local and general analgesic when chewed and the bark contains a substance (pukateine) that has similar numbing properties to morphine but without the associated side effects.

Pukatea has also been a preferred timber for Māori carving. Though not particularly durable in contact with the ground, the wood is lightweight and very strong with the added advantage of being both fire resistant and extremely hard to split. Indeed, because of its ability to take nails driven into it from any direction, it makes good planking for boats. It was used in housebuilding as weatherboards and external roofing. Thanks to its attractive yellow to greenish-brown colouring, the wood has always been well regarded by cabinetmakers and woodturners.

Although in natural surroundings it often reaches an immense height, pukatea grows only slowly in cultivation and so remains a manageable tree for specimen planting. Grows happily in wet ground even down to the water's edge. Raised either from seed or semi-hardwood cuttings. Prefers a deep, rich soil.

17

Makomako
Wineberry
Aristotelia serrata

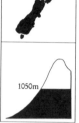

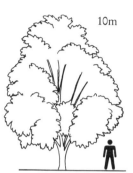

10m

1050m

Leaves: *opposite* (unlike houhere), deep teeth, *red stalks*, usually *reddish underneath*

Flowers: in late spring, small and pinkish-red

Fruit: in late summer (female trees only), small, dark red to black

Other: most common in regrowth forest

Nature Notes: fruit a favourite of tui and silvereye. Wood pigeon eat both fruit and leaves. In the North Island, holes in the trunk are likely to be the larval tunnels of the pūriri moth.

Uses: As the European name suggests, makomako berries were once used for making a wine, which at least one writer recommended as being 'first-rate'. The fruit were eaten raw by early Māori and made by later settlers into jellies and jams. Their taste varies from sweet to decidedly bitter. Liquid from boiled leaves was applied to burns, boils, sore eyes and rheumatic pains. An infusion of the bark soaked in cold water was used for sore eyes and the bark boiled to make a bath for rheumatic patients.

Again it was the bark that Māori bruised and steeped in hot water to produce a blue-black dye for colouring flax leaves. With the use of an alum mordant or bichromate of potash, modern homespinners have similarly produced shades of fawn. Māori even used the bark for making simple water containers.

Once occasionally used for fence rails, woodturning and marquetry, the timber's main use has been in making charcoal for the manufacture of certain kinds of gunpowder.

Attractive as a flowering specimen or background tree, makomako also gives quick and light shade for the growing of other plants – a function it fulfils just as well in the garden as in the natural regeneration of damaged forest. Grows easily from seed or stem cuttings and transplants easily.

Porokaiwhiri
Pigeonwood
Hedycarya arborea

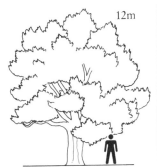

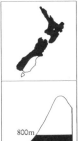

Leaves: *opposite* (unlike māhoe), dark glossy green above, paler below, *very widely spaced teeth*

Fruit: in late spring and early summer (female trees only), in bunches, orange-red

Trunk: bark dark brown, fairly smooth

Other: new branchlets furry brown

Nature Notes: as its European name suggests, the fruit is popular with wood pigeon. A pretty, well camouflaged, noctuid moth (wingspan 3.5cm) is sometimes seen on the trunk.

Uses: Porokaiwhiri is not particularly noticeable in the bush until around November when the otherwise inconspicuous flowers of the male trees produce a delightfully sweet fragrance, and even more so in early summer when its bunches of bright orange-red fruit appear. These fruit, though eaten in large quantities by wood pigeons, do not appear to be edible to humans – at least there is no record of their ever having been eaten by Māori. Indeed, tests conducted on the tree show that some parts may even be poisonous.

Medicinally, it was used by Māori in vapour baths, though more precise details were never recorded. No special uses of the soft, white, straight-grained wood are known.

Its erect shape, the fragrance of its blossoms, the bright colour of its fruit and its attractiveness to native birds all make porokaiwhiri a worthwhile specimen tree, especially in larger gardens or in parks. It requires some shelter from winds and protection from frosts while young, and is best planted in a good, rather deep, moist soil. Remember, if you want the trees to produce fruit, plant trees of both sexes. Grows easily from seed but can also be grown from semi-hardwood cuttings.

Kohekohe

Dysoxylum spectabile

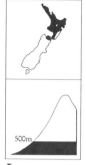

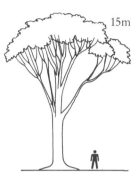

15m

500m

Leaves: *in 3 or 4 opposite pairs,* dark and shiny

Flowers: in early winter, long drooping sprays, white, growing directly from trunk or branches

Fruit: in late autumn, round green capsule, 2.5cm across, splitting to reveal orange-red centre

Trunk: *buttress roots* at base

Nature Notes: dying out in some areas due to possum damage. Bellbirds eat the nectar.

Uses: The astringent, orange-red pulp of the fruit was eaten by those with pulmonary tuberculosis to relieve blood-spitting, but generally it was the bark and leaves that were used medicinally. Both taste bitter and were regarded as an effective tonic – they are reported to have once been ingredients of home-made beer. Among the long list of healing properties attributed to them are the use of the brewed bark and leaves to relieve coughing, the gargled tea made from the leaves to soothe sore throats and a brew incorporating the bark for haemorrhages.

Chemical analysis of the heartwood has since revealed catechin, effective against diarrhoea and throat infections. The heartwood and bark are high in tannin (effective against haemorrhaging) and contain a compound (B-sitosterol) which can lower blood cholesterol levels.

Kohekohe wood, though now rather scarce, was once used by Māori for canoes, later by furniture makers and for fenceposts in well-drained sand. Wood from the odd wind-fallen tree is still highly valued for carving. Homespinners have made a grey dye from kohekohe using a chrome mordant, presumably by using the bark from fallen trees.

Frost tender and needs reasonable shelter but makes a very attractive specimen tree. Grown either from seed or cuttings.

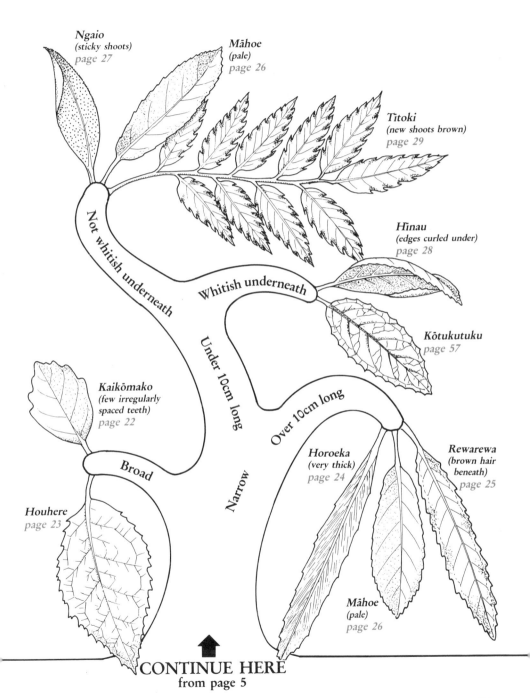

Ngaio
(sticky shoots)
page 27

Māhoe
(pale)
page 26

Titoki
(new shoots brown)
page 29

Hinau
(edges curled under)
page 28

Not whitish underneath

Whitish underneath

Kōtukutuku
page 57

Under 10cm long

Over 10cm long

Kaikōmako
(few irregularly
spaced teeth)
page 22

Broad

Narrow

Horoeka
(very thick)
page 24

Rewarewa
(brown hair
beneath)
page 25

Houhere
page 23

Māhoe
(pale)
page 26

CONTINUE HERE
from page 5

from page 5

21

Kaikōmako

Pennantia corymbosa

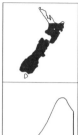
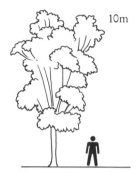

Leaves: alternating or clustered, 3–10cm long (less on young trees), *irregular widely spaced teeth*, thick

Flowers: in early summer, small, 5-petalled, creamy white, fragrant and profuse

Fruit: in early autumn (female trees only), small and black

Trunk: grey, sometimes with sooty mould

Nature Notes: fruit popular with whitehead and bellbird. Bees collect nectar September to December.

Uses: Kōmako is one of the Māori names for the bellbird, hence kaikōmako: food of the bellbird.

It was from Mahuika, the goddess of fire, that Māui learnt the secret of making fire with kaikōmako. The wood is so hard that a thoroughly dry and sharply pointed kaikōmako stick can be scraped along the grain of a dry slab of māhoe or patē, making a groove that fills with fine dust. This dust accumulates gradually at the end of the groove and, if the scraping is vigorous enough, will eventually start to smoke. With skill, patience and dedicated fanning, this smouldering dust will catch alight.

Its very hard, durable wood was once recommended for the likes of chisel handles but other than this was not much used except for an occasional, attractively marked piece chosen for woodturning or for ornamental detail in furniture making. Dead twigs make good kindling.

In its slender, mature form with its appealing summer flowers, kaikōmako makes a good specimen tree particularly suited to small gardens, though at the tangled, young stage, it can look quite scraggly. Grows easily from seed but semi-hardwood cuttings from the adult tree will shortcut the juvenile stage altogether and produce a flowering specimen at a younger age.

Houhere Lacebark

Hoheria populnea

Leaves: *alternating* (unlike makomako), 5–12cm long, large sharp teeth

Flowers: late summer/autumn, large, white, star-like

Other: *young branches grooved.* Other kinds of lacebark have different shaped leaves. All have white flowers and tend to grow along forest edges.

Nature Notes: pūriri moth caterpillars often tunnel into the trunk. Large, woody lumps (galls) seen on the stems are made by mites. Leaves are a winter food for wood pigeon. Bees collect nectar, especially in May.

Uses: In a mature houhere, just beneath the outside bark, is a layer of lacy, matted fibres 2–3cm thick and this gives the tree its European name. An important fibre source for early Māori, strips of the inner bark were twisted into rope and even beaten to make felted bark sheets similar to the tapa cloth of the Pacific Islands. Thin strips were made into headbands and flat plaits were woven like straw into broad-brimmed hats once admired for their softness and light weight. One such bonnet drew attention for its beauty while on display at the 1885 Wellington Exhibition and Princess Te Puea Herangi was to be seen wearing one regularly to the time of her death in 1952.

Māori made a jelly by soaking the inner bark in cold water and used it both externally for sore and weak eyes and internally for soothing the digestive system.

That the tree tends not to grow in large, pure stands has no doubt helped save it from the fate suffered by many of our tawa and beech forests, for the wood is similarly suitable for papermaking (and makes good firewood too).

The profusion of houhere's showy, white flowers in late summer and autumn make this one of our most popular garden trees. Grows well from seed (collected in May) or from semi-hardwood cuttings. Takes the occasional pruning.

This now includes what was known as *Hoheria sexstylosa.*

Horoeka
Lancewood
Pseudopanax crassifolius

Leaves: alternating, with teeth. On young trees 30cm (or more) long, on adult trees 7–20cm (can be toothless), *central rib and underside pale*

Fruit: autumn/winter (female trees only), 4–5mm, purplish-black

Trunk: spindly and sinewy like rope when young

Nature Notes: whitehead, tui, and wood pigeon feed on the fruit. Bees very common on the inconspicuous flowers in late February. The caterpillar of a leaf miner moth often tunnels the inside of leaves.

Uses: In spite of a straight and often spindly, branchless trunk and the tree's common European name, lancewood does not appear to have been used as a lance or spear.

This is clearly one of the most unusual trees of native forests, especially while still at a young age when its narrow, lance-like leaves can be over one metre in length. In one of the greatest transformations to take place between juvenile and adult tree, horoeka's juvenile leaves are replaced by ones often less than half their original length, and around twice their immature width.

The midribs of these young leaves are surprisingly strong and supple when fresh and were used by forest settlers as bootlaces and for mending bridles and harnesses. The straight, flexible, pole-like trunks were sometimes cut for use as stock and horse whips.

As a source of timber, horoeka appears to have been most used in Otago. Although not as durable as some woods, piles supporting the first jetty built at Port Chalmers around 1850 lasted intact for 30 years.

A popular garden tree or tub plant particularly in its juvenile stage, which it retains for 15–20 years. Grows easily from fresh, ripe seed (collected when the fruit is soft).

Rewarewa
New Zealand Honeysuckle
Knightia excelsa

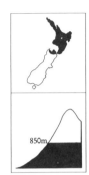

Leaves: long, stiff, with widely spaced teeth, *undersides, midvein and new growth velvety brown*, (seedling leaves longer)

Flowers: in late spring, in clusters, velvety, brick red in bud, peeling back to reveal yellow centres

Seeds: in summer, in long rusty brown pods

Nature Notes: nectar eaten by bellbird, silvereye, tui and bees. A large, beautifully iridescent weevil (15mm) can often be knocked out of the tree in early summer.

Uses: In regrowth forest especially, rewarewa is conspicuous for its poplar-like form poking through the scrub canopy. Otherwise its unusual, velvety, red and yellow flowers are noticed when they fall on the ground in late spring. To Māori, the appearance of these signalled the sixth month of their calendar (November).

The nectar used to be collected by Māori to eat; the picked flowers would be tapped on the inside of a gourd vessel. Nowadays, it is collected instead by introduced bees which produce from it an unusually dark and rich flavoured honey.

The inner bark was bandaged over a wound to stop bleeding and speed its healing.

Rewarewa's rather dark, flecked wood has been put to a number of decorative uses: tables, writing desks, picture frames, stationery cases etc, though nowadays more sparingly in woodturning and veneer work. It is so useless as firewood as to earn the settlers' nickname 'bucket of water tree'.

Recommended as a specimen tree suitable for any medium-sized garden. Hardy enough to grow as far south as Invercargill (along the coast at least). Will grow in very dry ground and tolerates both sun and shade but prefers a good, well drained, friable soil and plenty of light. Easily raised from fresh seed.

25

Māhoe
Whiteywood
Melicytus ramiflorus

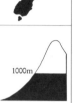

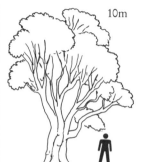

10m

1000m

Leaves:	*alternating* (unlike porokaiwhiri), with teeth
Flowers:	in early summer, small, greenish-yellow, sweet scented, grow direct from branches
Fruit:	in late summer (female trees only) small, purple
Trunk:	smooth, *white lichen patches*
Other:	very common in regrowth and coastal bush

Nature Notes: tui, silvereye and whitehead feed on the fruit. Bees collect both nectar and pollen.

Uses: To early Māori māhoe was perhaps most valued for its use in the friction method of fire lighting. Soft and easily kindled when dry, a slab of māhoe was one of the best woods for scraping with a pointed stick of a harder wood such as kaikōmako or tōtara (see kaikōmako for details).

To early Pākehā, it was most useful in the production of charcoal to make certain kinds of gunpowder; the timber itself is very brittle and plain and hence not much use except as firewood. Partly because it is so easy to find, māhoe is recommended by modern woodturners as a good practice timber when turned green and then dried in a micro-wave oven.

Māori used liquid from the boiled leaves externally for rheumatism and scabies, and the inner bark was frayed and applied as a pack to burns. To farmers māhoe leaves have provided emergency fodder for cattle and horses during extreme dry spells. Homespinners have used the leaves with an alum mordant for producing a dull green dye.

In cultivation māhoe is recommended for specimen planting in large gardens as fast growing shade and for its attractiveness to birds. Does best in a sheltered position, but will tolerate wind. Grows well from seed or semi-hardwood cuttings.

Ngaio

Myoporum laetum

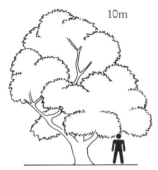

Leaves: when held up to the light, *pale dot-like oil glands* are visible; small teeth toward the tip

Flowers: in late spring and early summer, small, white, with purple spots

Fruit: in early autumn, small, reddish-purple

Other: *sticky black leaf buds*

Nature Notes: bees collect pollen and nectar, and use the sticky gum found on the buds in their hive construction. The fruit is eaten by several native birds.

Uses: Māori used to wash exposed parts of their bodies with an infusion of ngaio leaves or simply rub themselves with its sticky black shoots – either treatment would prevent mosquitoes and sandflies from biting.

The ripe, reddish-purple fruit were sometimes eaten by Māori but often taste quite bitter. They are in any case best left alone since the whole plant is now known to contain a substance (ngaione) that is toxic to the liver. This compound has fungicidal and bactericidal properties too which may explain some of the many external medicinal uses to which the leaves and bark have been put. The leaves, for example, when bruised and warmed to release their oil, were used as a poultice for septic wounds – a remedy which proved so effective that it was later used by veterinarians on horses. Ngaio leaves have also been used for making sheep dip.

A relatively small tree, ngaio's main timber uses have been limited to furniture making and woodturning, for which it is still valued today.

Mostly planted as a shelter tree particularly near the sea where it is found naturally. Can be trimmed, so makes a suitable hedge plant. When given enough space, its gnarled growth and spreading head make it a good specimen tree. Frost tender when young. Usually grown from seed but can be grown from cuttings.

Hīnau

Elaeocarpus dentatus

15m

600m

Leaves: 6–10cm long, *whitish under-neath*, small bumps along top surface, small teeth along *curled* edges

Flowers: in late spring, drooping, bell-shaped, white

Fruit: in early autumn, 12mm long, purplish when ripe

Trunk: greyish

Nature Notes: wood pigeon eat the fruit. Bees collect the nectar in October/November.

Uses: When hīnau bloomed, it was said by Tūhoe Māori to be time to burn off the bracken fern fronds to improve the crop to be had from the fern's edible roots. The bark (or rather a decoction of it in a hot bath) was believed to cure even the worst cases of skin disease and also provided Māori's main source of black dye, used with a black mud mordant for colouring flax. Likewise, an exudation taken from the tree was used to make a black pigment for tattooing. Its bark was also fashioned into simple water containers.

Most important of all to Māori though was the use of the thin flesh of the berries as food. The large stones are hard and quite inedible but the soft surrounding pulp was shaped into pudding-like cakes and cooked hāngi-style for two hours or more. Although once popular, it is rarely, if ever, eaten nowadays.

With an average tannin content of over 7%, hīnau bark became an important raw material in the mid-19th century for the local leather tanning industry. Today, the bark is used by handcraft enthusiasts to yield (depending on the mordant) greenish-fawn, light greenish-brown and sage green dyes. Some enterprising children have even used this bark to make a writing ink.

Its bell-shaped flowers make hīnau an attractive garden tree. Easy to grow from seed.

Tītoki

Alectryon excelsus

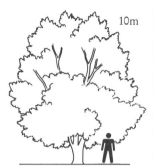

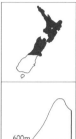

Leaves: alternating to almost opposite, *in 4–6 pairs*, mostly without teeth, *new growth with brown fur*

Fruit: in early summer; hard, brown seed case, splits to reveal large shiny black seed in juicy red pulp

Other: most common on river flats

Nature Notes: wood pigeon and other birds eat the fruit. Caterpillars of a small, white moth sometimes chew out the inside of the leaves. In summer, small, dark, native bronze beetles (5mm) chew shot-like holes in the leaves.

Uses: Although early Māori occasionally ate the pulp of the fruit, it was the oil from the large, shiny, black seed that was most highly valued. And, no doubt, this is why they sometimes planted tītoki. Among its many uses, the oil served as a hair oil and even, on at least one occasion, as a lamp oil. When Captain Jean-Francois de Surville and his crew on the *St Jean Baptiste* visited in 1769–1770, they purchased this oil from local Māori for lighting in their ship.

The greenish oil was squeezed from the seeds by a process of crushing followed by the ingenious use of a tourniquet-style flax bag. If it were to be used as a hair oil, fragrant leaves or gums were later steeped in it. Medicinally, the oil was usually applied externally – for soothing and healing purposes. Later it was recommended as a lubricant suitable for use by watchmakers.

Today, the fruit is an ingredient of a liqueur currently exported to several countries.

Tītoki timber has been prized for its strength and elasticity by wheelwrights and coach-makers for a variety of uses. It also makes good axe handles.

Sensitive to frost and wind, but makes a good specimen tree. Easiest to grow from seed taken from mature capsules.

Tānekaha
Celery Pine
Phyllocladus trichomanoides

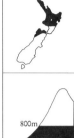

20m

Leaves: 1.5–2.5cm long, fan-like and leathery, together *looking like a celery leaf**

Trunk: smooth with grey patches

Other: *often quite symmetrical with branches in regular tiers.* (The more northern toatoa has larger 'leaves'. The more southern and high country mountain toatoa has smaller ones.)

Nature Notes: small, brown, waxy lumps made by a scale insect can sometimes be seen on new shoots and undersides of the 'leaves'.

Uses: In the late 19th century, tānekaha bark was exported in large quantities to Germany as a source of red and pink dyes and to London for use as an organic mordant in the manufacture of kid gloves. Young trees supplied straight, flexible rods, exported to London to make walking sticks.

Homespinners still use this bark for dyeing wool, producing, depending on the mordant used, pinky beige, henna, chestnut, khaki, yellow-brown, and brown. Early Māori pounded the bark and soaked flax garments and mats with this pulp in cold water, bringing the whole mixture to the boil by throwing in hot stones to produce a red-brown dye. They used the bark too as a remedy for dysentery (effective no doubt because of its exceptionally high tannin content) and occasionally as a material for making simple water containers.

Tānekaha timber has been put to a great range of uses, from the manufacture of threshing machines to mine props and fish hooks. Its remarkable flexibility makes it especially suitable for fishing rods and the like.

In cultivation it forms an attractively symmetrical specimen tree and is fairly fast growing. Hard to propagate from cuttings, and only slightly easier from fresh seed.

---

*Although they look like leaves, technically they are a flattened stem.

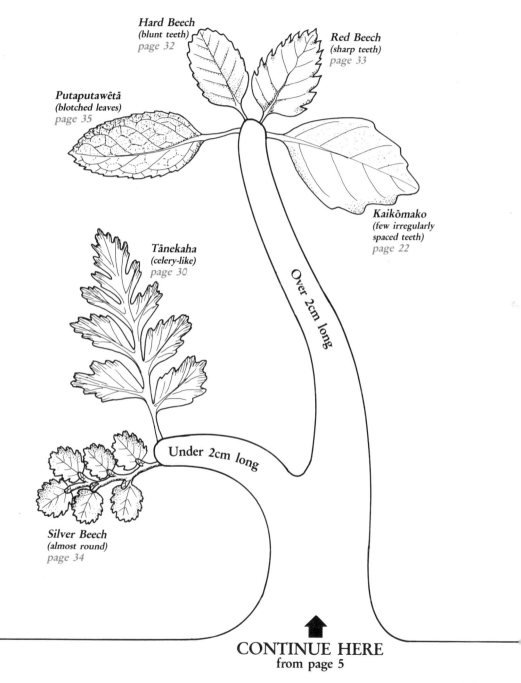

Hard Beech
(blunt teeth)
page 32

Red Beech
(sharp teeth)
page 33

Putaputawētā
(blotched leaves)
page 35

Kaikōmako
*(few irregularly
spaced teeth)*
page 22

Tānekaha
(celery-like)
page 30

Over 2cm long

Under 2cm long

Silver Beech
(almost round)
page 34

CONTINUE HERE
from page 5

Tawhai Raunui
Hard Beech

Nothofagus truncata

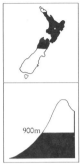

30m

Leaves: *alternating* (unlike kāmahi), *blunt* teeth (unlike red beech), *4 or more veins* each side of central vein (unlike silver beech), 2.5–4cm long, thick, loses many of its leaves in early spring

Trunk: often buttressed at base, bark thick, furrowed, grey

Nature Notes: honeydew sometimes found on the trunk attracts various birds and insects and provides food for a sooty mould.

Differences: Hard beech and red beech are very similar. Not only do they share the same Māori name, but early botanists believed them to be the same tree. In fact, the only sure way to tell the difference is to look on the underside of a leaf. If it has one or more small, furry, light brown spots where the first side veins meet the central vein of the leaf, then it is a red beech. If not, it is a hard beech.

Uses: Like the other beeches, hard beech apparently had no specific Māori use, but the timber was put to a variety of uses by later settlers.

In the late 19th century, it was highly thought of for railway sleepers, marine piles, mine props, and in housebuilding for piles, framing, floor joists and weatherboards. Of the native beeches, its timber is the most durable and is, as the name suggests, the hardest. However, silica in the wood rays has a drastic blunting effect on saws, chisels and power tools, making it an unpopular wood for turning and furniture making.

Hard beech is the only native beech commonly found growing north of Auckland. Considered a handsome tree, suitable for specimen planting where there is space, it grows easily from seed (collected in summer), provided the seed is fresh.

Tawhai Raunui
Red Beech

Nothofagus fusca

30m

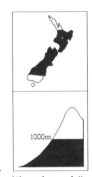

1000m

Leaves: *alternating* (unlike kāmahi), 2.5–4cm long, large *sharp* teeth (unlike other beech), bright red on young trees in winter, undersides with *furry yellowish spot* where first side veins meet central vein

Trunk: often buttressed, mostly smooth

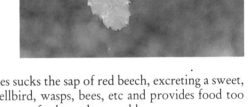

Nature Notes: a scale insect sometimes sucks the sap of red beech, excreting a sweet, sticky honeydew which attracts kākā, bellbird, wasps, bees, etc and provides food too for a soot-like mould. Fungus beetles in turn feed on the mould.

Uses: Red beech gets its common name either from the colour of its wood or from the colour of the leaves of young trees in winter – a feature which gives the tree a deciduous appearance. In large areas of South Island forest it is the dominant tree, often forming attractive avenues along some roads in Fiordland and Nelson Province.

Perhaps the only specific use of the tree by Māori is as a source of black dye used to colour fibres like flax and cabbage tree leaves. Later, its bark was used by settlers for tanning leather. The honeydew found on the trunks has long been of use to beekeepers either as a winter bee food or harvested for export.

As a timber tree it has been put to much the same uses as hard beech – railway sleepers, mine props, house construction, wharves and bridges. Though sawn timber is particularly slow to dry, when properly dried it is selected for boatbuilding and furniture making.

In cultivation, this is the most versatile of the native beeches, particularly good as a specimen tree in parks and large lawns. Can be clipped as a hedge or shelter tree or grown in a container. Grows readily from seed (collected in summer), so long as the seed is fresh.

Tawhai
Silver Beech

Nothofagus menziesii

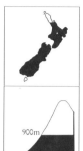

30m

900m

Leaves: *roundish*, 8–12mm (unlike other beech), with *rounded double teeth*

Trunk: often buttressed, bark of young trees have horizontal cracks, bark of older trees rough and flaking

Other: young shoots covered in brown hairs

Nature Notes: the honeydew and fungus common on other beeches is rare on silver beech. A parasitic mistletoe with red flowers (around Christmas) is sometimes seen. Also three kinds of 'beech strawberry', the prettiest of which is a round, orange, honeycombed fungus about 3cm across.

Uses: Named for the silvery white bark of younger trees, silver beech was used by Māori to produce a black dye for colouring cabbage tree and flax leaves. Later, it was the principal source of bark used by at least one leather tannery in Nelson – the air-dried bark containing around 7% tannin.

As a timber tree, though strong, it was found unsuitable for use in places where it would be exposed to weather. It is, however, one of New Zealand's better timbers for steam-bending and was bent into shape by coopers for making tubs, baskets and wine casks. For its attractive grain and colouring (pale pink to deep red), it was in steady demand around the turn of the century for making 'French bedsteads' and sideboards. Nowadays it remains a popular timber for the woodturner's craft – a far more appropriate use than woodchipping for export to pulp and paper manufacturers.

Although not commonly planted, it makes an appealing specimen tree especially while young. Can also be grown in decorative containers for patios and decks. Unlike the other beeches, it doesn't shed large quantities of leaves in winter or spring. Grows easily from fresh seed (best collected in late summer).

Putaputawētā
Marbleleaf

Carpodetus serratus

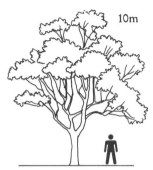

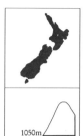

Leaves: small, with sharp teeth, *yellowish blotches between veins*

Flowers: in early summer, small, star-like, white, in clusters, with a sweet scent

Fruit: in early autumn, round, small, black capsule

Other: young trees form a tangled shrub with much smaller leaves on zigzag branches

Nature Notes: in the North Island, the trunk is usually full of holes made by the pūriri moth caterpillar. These later provide homes for wētā.

Uses: The tree's beautifully lilting name refers to the wētā that are so commonly found living in holes in the trunks of North Island trees. The holes are tunnelled by the caterpillar of the giant green pūriri moth and when they abandon them, the wētā take over. A more common feature on South Island putaputawētā is a parasitic native mistletoe called pirita.

No traditional Māori use of the tree is known, but homespinners have put the ripe, black fruit to use for colouring wool. With a chrome mordant it produces a soft green dye.

The white, open-grained wood, though not durable in contact with the ground, is strong, tough and elastic, making it a prized timber of the early bushmen and settlers for axe and other tool handles, and fence rails. It has sometimes been used in furniture making though not apparently by modern carvers or cabinetmakers. The wood is generally too sappy to provide a useful firewood.

Can be used as part of a shrub border or as a specimen or small canopy tree to provide moderate shelter and shade for other plants. Prefers a good, deep soil. Easily grown from ripe seed (collected when the fruit is soft) though semi-hardwood cuttings from the adult tree shortcut the scraggly juvenile stage.

Kōwhai
Sophora microphylla

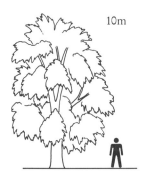

10m

Leaves: small, round, in *20–40 pairs*, (another kōwhai has fewer, longer leaves), loses most of its leaves in winter

Flowers: in early spring, large, drooping, bright yellow

Seeds: in winter, in a long brown pea-like pod

Other: shoots and branchlets furry brown

Nature Notes: nectar a favourite of bees, tui and bellbird. Wood pigeon eat the leaves and petals. The small, grey-green caterpillar of the kōwhai moth feeds on the leaves.

Uses: Appropriately, kōwhai is the Māori word for the colour yellow and its flowers make this one of our most showy and attractive native trees. Not surprising then that it was (in 1783) one of the first New Zealand plants to appear in London plant catalogues. However, it has no need of people to distribute itself; kōwhai seeds can stay afloat and viable over huge distances, which explains why 'our national flower' grows also in Chile and on distant Gough Island in the South Atlantic.

Kōwhai's flowering marked for some Māori the time to plant kūmara, its wood provided handles for axes and the bark, inner bark, flowers, leaves and juice of the roots were all used medicinally. (Experimentation is not recommended on account of the toxic alkaloids in all parts of the tree.)

Plant dye enthusiasts collect the petals to obtain an 'excellent' yellow with an alum mordant, and gold with bichromate of potash.

The timber is strong, durable and elastic with a range of uses which included making the teeth and bows of the old style hay rake. Bows a mere 6mm in diameter could be bent into a 23cm semicircle without the slightest sign of giving way.

Grows easily from fresh seed or semi-hardwood cuttings. Chip old seeds first with a knife or cover with boiling water and soak overnight.

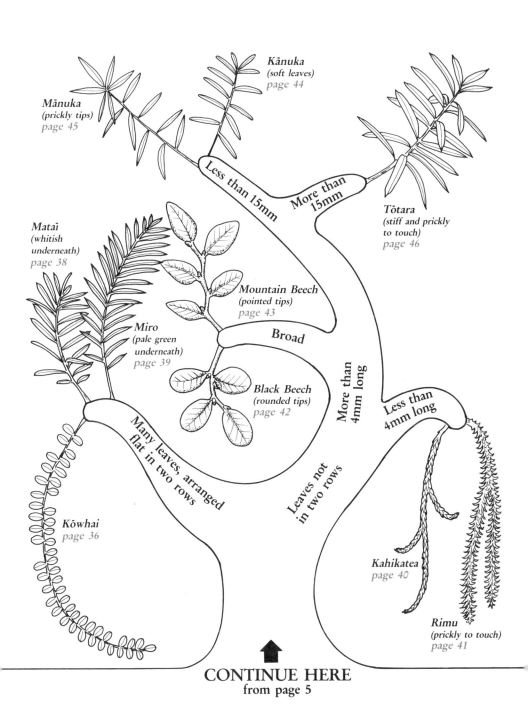

Mānuka
(prickly tips)
page 45

Kānuka
(soft leaves)
page 44

Less than 15mm

More than 15mm

Tōtara
(stiff and prickly to touch)
page 46

Matai
(whitish underneath)
page 38

Mountain Beech
(pointed tips)
page 43

Miro
(pale green underneath)
page 39

Broad

Black Beech
(rounded tips)
page 42

More than 4mm long

Less than 4mm long

Many leaves, arranged flat in two rows

Leaves not in two rows

Kōwhai
page 36

Kahikatea
page 40

Rimu
(prickly to touch)
page 41

CONTINUE HERE
from page 5

37

Mataī

Prumnopitys taxifolia

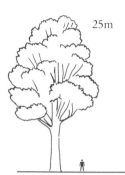

25m

500m

Leaves: arranged in two rows (unlike tōtara), slightly scraggly, *bluish-white underneath* (unlike miro), with a strong smell when crushed, over 1cm long (unlike young kahikatea)

Fruit: in summer (female trees only), blue-black, round

Trunk: hammer marked on mature trees

Nature Notes: bees collect pollen from the small, yellow catkins October-November. Fruit popular with wood pigeon and kākā. A leaf tyer caterpillar sometimes makes a messy nest in the leaves.

Uses: Mataī's round, black fruit were eaten raw by early Māori. They taste sweet though quite slimy. When mataī was still being felled in quantity for its timber, bushmen drilled the base of standing trees with an auger to collect a sap they called mataī beer. The hole was then plugged and tapped like a barrel. If taken at the right stage, the beer was said to be sweet and refreshing with a bitter aftertaste, and reportedly was effective against pulmonary tuberculosis.

Mataī is one of the timbers traditionally used for Māori carving and has since been recommended for making musical instruments. Because of its strength, durability and its hardwearing and non-dent properties, it was frequently chosen for the floors of churches, schools, ballrooms and the like. These days it still gets used for furniture and woodturning, table and bench tops, window sills and doorsteps.

The bark has a relatively low tannin content but was occasionally used by leather tanneries, and more recently to produce a brown or mushroom dye for colouring wool. The wood contains matairesinol, proven effective in reducing cancer in mice.

Grown from ripe seed but cuttings from the adult tree will circumvent the scraggly juvenile stage.

Miro

Prumnopitys ferruginea

25m

1000m

Leaves: arranged in 2 rows (unlike tōtara), *curved, pale green below* (unlike mataī), strong smell when crushed, over 1.5cm long (unlike young kahikatea)

Fruit: throughout the year (female trees only), 2cm long, pinkish-purple

Trunk: hammer marked on mature trees

Nature Notes: bees collect pollen from the yellow catkins in September and October. The fruit is a favourite of wood pigeon and kākā, especially in autumn to early winter.

Uses: The ripe, pinkish-purple fruit was eaten raw by early Māori. It tastes and smells like turpentine but has some sweetness too – definitely an acquired taste. However, they are clearly a favourite of the wood pigeon which eat them in vast quantities.

The aromatic oil squeezed from the fruit was used by early Māori too as a body perfume. It was also taken internally to reduce fevers and when rubbed on the skin was reputed to have the added benefit of acting as an insecticide. A gum from the bark placed on wounds is apparently good for stopping bleeding and to heal ulcers. For gonorrhoea an infusion of leaves and bark was taken and for stomach-ache an infusion of the bark alone.

Miro bark was also one of the materials used by Māori for water containers. Home-spinners have produced brown, maroon and mushroom shades from it depending on the mordant used.

The timber proved valuable for marine piling and house framing, floors and weather-boards, but it is not durable in contact with the ground. Nowadays it is used for some furniture making, woodturning and carving.

Attractive for specimen planting. Withstands clipping and can be used as a slow-growing hedge. Grown from seed or cuttings, though seeds can take up to two years to germinate.

Kahikatea
White Pine
Dacrycarpus dacrydioides

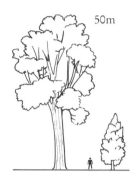

50m

600m

Leaves: scale-like, overlapping, (in 2 rows on young growth), *soft to touch* (unlike rimu)

Fruit: in autumn (female trees only), black seed on a juicy orange-red base

Trunk: paint-like bands when young, later grey and flaking

Other: common in swampy forest; young branches tend to turn upwards

Nature Notes: fruit is popular with wood pigeon, kākā and tui. Bees collect a white pollen from the catkins in September and October.

Uses: The juicy, orange-red base that holds the kahikatea seed was an important food of early Māori. At one feast, for example, 60 baskets of this fruit (along with 136 pigs) were served. They are sweet with a slight piney aftertaste.

A tonic medicine was made by leaving chips of the wood to steep in boiling water and drinking the liquid; the podocarpic acid the tree contains is known to encourage the flow of bile.

For making bird spears, kahikatea was the favoured wood and the soot obtained from burning the heartwood supplied a pigment for tattooing.

Newer settlers put the timber to a range of indoor uses. But by far the biggest use of the wood was in the period from 1885 to the 1940s in the making of parchment-lined butter boxes. Being odourless, clean-looking and lightweight, kahikatea proved the ideal material. As our butter left these shores by the 56lb slab, so too did the vast majority of our kahikatea stands.

Our tallest native tree, it is also believed to be our most ancient, with pollen remains dating back over 100 million years.

A fine specimen tree, especially in wet or swampy areas. Grows easily and quickly from seed, but cuttings from mature trees will shortcut the less attractive juvenile stage.

40

Rimu

Dacrydium cupressinum

35m

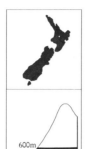

600m

Leaves: scale-like, overlapping, *prickly to touch* (unlike kahikatea)

Fruit: mostly in autumn (female trees only), black seed in juicy red cup (not common)

Trunk: dark brown, peeling in large flakes

Other: branches gracefully weeping

Nature Notes: occasionally seen on the trunk is the black and brown elephant weevil (1–2cm long) with its characteristic trunk-like snout.

Uses: It seems surprising that homebrewers have not yet discovered rimu beer. Captain Cook was even thoughtful enough to record the recipe for this highly esteemed and apparently healthy beverage: boil young rimu and mānuka branches for 3–4 hours, strain and add molasses (10 gallons of it, if, like him, you are brewing 240 gallons), bring to the boil, add an equal quantity of cold water, leave to cool and add yeast.

The juicy, red cup that holds the rimu seed was eaten by Māori and the inner bark pulped to put on burns. The bitter gum was used to stem bleeding and the leaves used on sores. To these traditional uses, modern chemical analysis has added a new one: the podocarpic acid found in the heartwood can increase the flow of bile.

Rimu heartwood is so resinous that it was split into shreds and tied in bundles by Māori for use as torches.

For the new settlers rimu became the main building timber in areas where kauri did not grow, and its bark became a common source of tannin for tanning certain qualities of leather. Today, a brown dye is occasionally made from the bark using an alum mordant, and the wood is still used for furniture, woodturning and carving.

Rimu makes a graceful garden tree. Usually grown from seed but also from erect-growing, semi-hardwood cuttings. Slow to germinate and slow growing too. Difficult to transplant beyond seedling stage.

Tawhai Rauriki
Black Beech

Nothofagus solandri

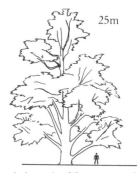

25m

750m

Leaves: *rounded tip* (unlike mountain beech), *no teeth* (unlike red, hard and silver beech), 1–1.5cm long

Flowers: in spring, tiny, give the tree a distinct reddish colour

Trunk: bark pale and smooth on young trees, black and furrowed on old trees

Nature Notes: common in northern South Island is a scale insect that sucks the sap, leaving a sticky honeydew – a food for wasps, butterflies, bees, tui, kākā, bellbird, silvereye, kea, possums and a soot-like mould.

Uses: Though 'honeydew' honey from the black beech forests of northeastern South Island appears to go more or less unappreciated in New Zealand, it supplies Canterbury beekeepers with a prized export. Here, it was used as far back as the early 1930s as a component of a well known cough mixture.

In the 19th century the bark was selected for its high tannin content, and crushed along with the bark of silver beech to make a brew for tanning leather. The wood was used greatly for bridges, beams and decking, flooring and wall panelling, railway sleepers, gateposts, fence rails and cartwheel spokes. Indeed, it was once the major building material in Canterbury. Though stable enough when dry for use in furniture making and wood-turning, it contains large quantities of silica which quickly blunts tools.

Sadly, large areas of remaining beech forest are these days being clear-felled to make woodchips for pulping by foreign papermakers.

Where space allows, black beech can make an attractive specimen tree, with the advantage over most other beeches of being more resistant to wind damage. Grows well from seed (collected in late summer), so long as it is sown while still fresh.

Tawhai Rauriki
Mountain Beech

Nothofagus solandri var. *cliffortioides*

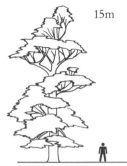

15m

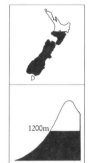

1200m

Leaves: *triangular, pointed* (unlike black beech), *edges curled under* (unlike black beech), *no teeth* (unlike red, hard and silver beech), about 1cm long, a few hairs on top surface

Trunk: smooth and dark

Nature Notes: especially in the northern South Island, a sap-sucking scale insect leaves honeydew on the tree – food for tui, kākā, kea, silvereye, bellbird, butterflies, bees, wasps and sustenance for a soot-like mould which is, in turn, food of fungus beetles.

Uses: It would seem from its native name that Māori did not distinguish between this and the very closely related black beech – not surprising since they are very similar. Indeed, telling the two apart is made even more difficult by the fact that the two trees frequently hybridise to produce a whole range of subtle variations.

As its European name suggests, it can grow in the most severe conditions high in the mountains, and yet in the south it does grow right down to sea level.

Although once often used for making gates, fences and floors, it is not as durable as black beech. Just as well perhaps since its removal from steep terrain would soon cause severe erosion and flooding. This protection of rugged, high country is without doubt the tree's most important 'use', but mountain beech also provides the sought-after beech honeydew, collected by South Island beekeepers for export to Europe.

A versatile tree, it is compact, fairly fast growing and probably the hardiest of all native beeches – able to withstand heavy frosts, snow and intense rainfall. Often grows in poor soil. Good for bonsai cultivation and in rock gardens. Seed ripe in early autumn.

Kānuka
White Tea Tree
Kunzea ericoides

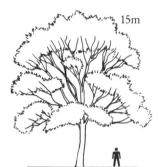

15m

900m

Leaves: about 1cm long, *soft to touch, no prickly tip* (unlike mānuka)

Flowers: in summer, profuse, very fragrant, white, in *clusters* (unlike mānuka), *less than* 6mm across (unlike mānuka)

Seeds: narrower, longer capsules than mānuka seeds

Trunk: grows taller than mānuka, thin peeling bark

Nature Notes: bees common on flowers in February. Kānuka longhorn beetles sometimes found on dead wood.

Uses: Of the wide range of medicinal properties attributed to kānuka, perhaps the most substantiated is the use of pounded seed capsules to make a poultice for running sores. (Essential oils from several members of this family are proven effective against the common bacterium *Staphylococcus aureus*.) Kānuka also contains leptospermone, an insecticide and an effective remedy for intestinal worms.

The better known use of kānuka (and mānuka) leaves for brewing tea is not a traditionally Māori one, but began with Captain Cook. A teaspoonful of fresh, young leaves per cup is plenty.

Early Māori did, however, value the timber highly for making the shafts of bird spears. They used its inner bark too as a durable and waterproof roofing material.

In more recent times, kānuka was not only favoured for the usual outdoor timber uses, like house and marine piles etc, but also for making the spokes of horse-drawn coaches and wagons, and for tool and implement handles. Of course it is good firewood too and this led (and still leads) to its complete destruction in many areas.

Its great mass of white flowers makes kānuka a good specimen tree, with the advantage of being resistant to the sooty mānuka blight. Grown from seed or semi-hardwood cuttings.

Mānuka
Tea Tree

Leptospermum scoparium

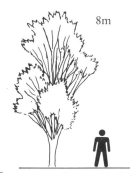

8m

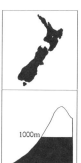

1000m

Leaves: about 1cm long, *stiff, tip prickly to touch* (unlike kānuka)

Flowers: most prolific in late spring, usually white (sometimes pink), *more than* 6mm across (unlike kānuka)

Seeds: in hard *broad* seed capsules (unlike kānuka)

Other: only grows to 8m high (unlike kānuka)

Nature Notes: bees feed on the nectar. Mānuka beetles (8mm, green or brown) are seen on the tree in early summer. The common sooty colouring is caused by the mānuka blight fungus growing on the honeydew of an Australian scale insect.

Uses: That Captain Cook and his crew brewed mānuka leaves to make tea* and beer is fairly well known, but many of the plant's other uses are not. It contains, for example, a compound (leptospermone) that acts as an insecticide and its essential oil has been recognised as an excellent perfume for soap-making.

Early Māori used its bark for making water containers and the inner bark as a waterproof layer for roofing and even the odd waterproof cape. Straight mānuka poles were used for battens and rafters in whare building, or made into bird spear shafts and paddles. A sweet, gum-like deposit found on the trunk provided food, the true gum was used for scenting hair oil, and the flexible seedlings for making crayfish traps.

More recent settlers cut mānuka twigs to make brooms, used the bark for dyeing wool (fawn to light brown), cut the stems for hop poles, tool and implement handles or quality firewood, used the sawdust for smoking fish, or lastly – but not least – left it standing as a nursery for regenerating forest. Hardly the useless weed many a farmer would have us believe. Grown from seed or semi-hardwood cuttings.

*'Ti Tree' is a misspelling confusing the tree's use as tea with the Māori name for cabbage tree.

Tōtara

Podocarpus totara

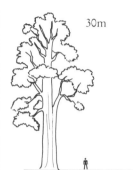

30m

Leaves: stiff, *prickly* to touch, *not in 2 rows* (unlike mataī and miro), up to 2.5cm long (seedlings longer)

Fruit: in autumn (female trees only), green seed, juicy red base

Trunk: stringy red-brown bark

Other: more common in the south and at higher altitudes is the longer-leaved Hall's tōtara

Nature Notes: tui feed on the fruit. Bees collect pollen in September–October. A pallid longhorn beetle (20mm x 2mm) is sometimes found on dead and dying twigs.

Uses: The huge Māori waka taua (war canoes), capable of carrying 100 warriors, were, and still are, often hollowed out from a single tōtara log. It has been the preferred wood for large carvings and framing for whare. The inner bark was used for roofing and for storage containers, and the outer bark as a splint to support fractured bones.

To produce fire by friction, a pointed tōtara stick could be scraped on a slab of softer wood such as māhoe (see kaikōmako for further details). Medicinally, both the smoke from the burning wood and the boiled bark were used. A valued food, Māori collected the bright red fruit (minus the seeds) by the basketload; they are sweet and juicy with a slightly piney flavour.

Huge areas of tōtara were felled to supply general building timber, railway sleepers, bridge and wharf timber and telephone poles. Nowadays, it is used largely for carving and furniture making. Homespinners have produced a wide range of browns and even a sage green dye from the bark.

When grown in the open as a specimen tree, the young tōtara bears branches and leaves right down to the ground. Can also be grown as a hedge plant. Grows easily from fresh seed or tip cuttings. Relatively fast growing, very hardy, tolerant of both wet and dry conditions, and will withstand wind.

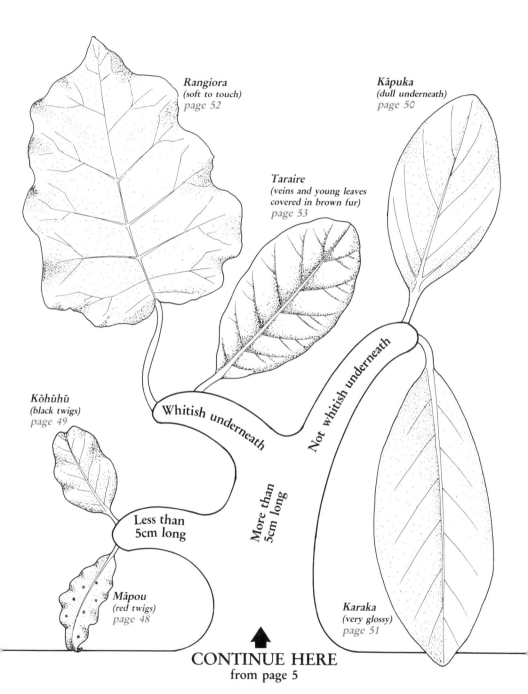

Rangiora
(soft to touch)
page 52

Kāpuka
(dull underneath)
page 50

Taraire
(veins and young leaves
covered in brown fur)
page 53

Kōhūhū
(black twigs)
page 49

Whitish underneath

Not whitish underneath

Less than
5cm long

More than
5cm long

Māpou
(red twigs)
page 48

Karaka
(very glossy)
page 51

CONTINUE HERE
from page 5

Māpou
Myrsine australis

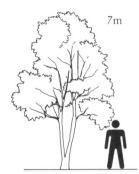

7m

Leaves: with distinctly *wavy edges*, reddish green on new growth, often with reddish spots (unlike kōhūhū), mostly 2–5cm long

Fruit: in summer, very small, almost black, borne on stem

Other: *young stems red* (unlike kōhūhū)

Nature Notes: fruit attracts silvereye, tui, whitehead and others. Leaves are sometimes webbed together by leaf roller caterpillars.

Uses: Although māpou leaves were boiled by early Māori to make an infusion for toothache, this does not seem to have been a common use. However, the leaves are known to contain rutin, used in the relief of arthritic problems. Māpou also contains embelin which has been used elsewhere as a remedy for skin disease, intestinal worms and as a general tonic. More common in New Zealand was Māori's ceremonial and magical use of a branch of the tree to perform karakia or incantations.

The pale, red-veined timber has been used by cabinetmakers both in solid form and as a veneer and, because of its strength, it was recommended for wooden chairs and the handles of chisels and other carpenter's tools. While not durable if left in contact with the ground, timber from the larger trees was sometimes used for rafters, beams and joists. Its most popular use, however, has probably been as firewood.

As a hardy tree or shrub that can take regular clipping and quite severe pruning, māpou is a popular hedge or shrub border plant, appreciated for its resistance to wind. Also suitable for planting as a specimen or background tree. A variegated form is available with greenish-yellow centres to the leaves. Grows easily from seed and can also be raised from semi-hardwood cuttings. Quick growing.

Kōhūhū

Pittosporum tenuifolium

8m

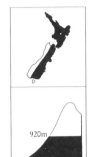

920m

Leaves: *3–6cm long* (unlike tarata), pleasant sweet smell when crushed, *often with wavy edges*

Flowers: in late spring, small, very dark red to almost black

Fruit: ripe in late autumn, round dark seed capsule, splits to reveal sticky black seeds

Other: *stalks dark or black* (unlike māpou)

Nature Notes: popular with bees for both nectar and pollen. Birds are attracted to the seeds.

Uses: Kōhūhū produces three distinct fragrances: one from the crushed leaf, one from the gum or broken branchlet and one from the flowers at night. Not surprising then that early Māori turned to this plant for making perfume. By bruising the bark or by making short, vertical cuts in it, they were able to collect the gum for scenting hair oil made from tītoki seed oil (see tītoki) or ointments made from wood pigeon fat. Leaves were used similarly in scent sachets.

The same gum was also mixed with the bitter dried sap of pūhā and chewed as a form of chewing gum. Kōhūhū found medicinal use for treating scabies, eczema of the scalp and other skin diseases (although which part of the tree was used remains unclear).

As a timber, it has the distinction of having almost twice the strength of English oak, though its lack of durability in the ground has limited its usefulness. Surprisingly, as a plant dye, it is the tiny flowers that are used and these produce a grass green (sounds like a lot of work!).

Useful grown as a shrub, hedge or small tree. Valued for its hardiness, attractive foliage, sweet flower scent, and to attract birds. Its use as a hedge plant has spread as far as Cornwall, England, where sprigs of kōhūhū are cut for sale in the London flower markets. At least a dozen cultivated varieties available. Best grown from seed.

49

Kāpuka/Pāpāuma
Broadleaf
Griselinea littoralis

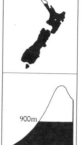

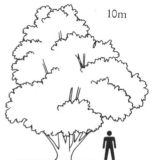

10m

900m

Leaves: often *slightly* unequal at base (on the closely related puka, the base is *very* unequal-sided), dark green on top, *never shiny below* (unlike karaka)

Fruit: in autumn (female trees only), very small, purple-black

Trunk: short and gnarled

Nature Notes: in spring, bees collect pollen from the tiny flowers. Large black and white striped longhorn beetles sometimes hide under the leaves. Tiny weevils chew out the insides of some leaves.

Uses: In times of food shortage, early Māori reportedly ate the tiny, ripe kāpuka berries, but they do taste decidedly bitter. The inner bark was used as a remedy for certain types of tuberculosis and sexually transmitted diseases.

In more recent times, plant dye enthusiasts have produced khaki and grey shades in wool with the use of an alum mordant (presumably by using the bark).

Kāpuka's red timber has been selected for its durability, especially for house piles, fenceposts and railway sleepers. The fact that it rarely has any length of straight trunk frustrated most timber workers though boatbuilders were able to turn this apparent drawback to their advantage.

As a garden tree or shrub, kāpuka offers attractive foliage and a remarkable tolerance to persistent winds and salt spray. As well, its ability to withstand heavy pruning has made it a popular hedge plant overseas, though oddly less so here. Grows easily from seed or semi-hardwood cuttings. A range of variegated varieties is also available.

Also widely cultivated, and often considered more attractive, is the closely related puka. This has larger, much glossier leaves very markedly unequal-sided where the base of the leaf meets the leaf stalk.

Karaka

Corynocarpus laevigatus

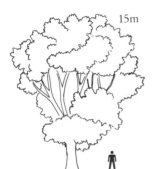

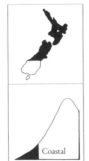

Leaves: dark green, *very glossy*, glossy beneath (unlike kāpuka), *edges tightly curled under* (unlike kāpuka), no teeth, large, 10–15cm long

Fruit: in summer, orange when ripe, 2.5–4cm long

Trunk: smooth and grey-brown

Nature Notes: fruit popular with wood pigeon. Bees feed on small flowers August–December. The long-snouted giraffe weevil inhabits the trunks of dying trees.

Uses: So important a food to early Māori were the properly prepared kernels of karaka berries, that this is one of the few trees they cultivated. In fact, according to Māori oral history (but contrary to current botanical knowledge), they brought the tree with them to Aotearoa.

Eaten raw, these kernels not only taste unpalatable but are **highly poisonous**, causing violent convulsions followed by permanent paralysis. Eaten, however, after several days' cooking and several weeks' soaking in a running stream, they taste rather like sweet chestnuts. In thermal areas, baskets of the ripe fruit were simply left in a boiling spring for about 18 hours and then carefully rinsed.

The leaves were said to be healing to wounds provided the upper surface was in contact with the wound; reversed, they drew out pus. Chemically, the kernels contain karakin, caronarian and cibarian, all of which are known to kill grass grub larvae – an effect which may have commercial application.

Although once used by Māori for making canoes, karaka wood is generally regarded as useless except for firewood.

Useful either as shelter or for its attractive foliage and large, orange fruit. Grows easily from fresh seed (which germinates quickly); variegated varieties are grown from semi-hardwood cuttings.

Rangiora

Brachyglottis repanda

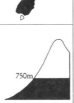

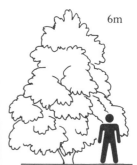

6m

Leaves: very large and soft, mostly 10–20cm long, *white beneath*, with wavy edges

Flowers: in spring, creamy white, in large bunches, sweet smelling

Other: the long leaf stalks are also white

Nature Notes: bees collect nectar in spring and occasionally in February a kind of honeydew is found on the trunks. Holes in the leaves are often made by large, hairy caterpillars (woolly bears). Their eggs appear under the leaves September–June.

Uses: The large, soft and slightly velvety leaves have earned the tree its popular European name, bushman's toilet paper. And very good it is too. But equally handy for those less well equipped for their tramp are the bright undersides of the leaves for use as notepaper.

The leaves' generous size and unusual flexibility were appreciated too by Māori, for such uses as wrapping hāngi meals and as lids to cover preserved food. In some places, at least, they appear to have cultivated a particularly broad-leaved form.

Māori applied the leaves to wounds and old ulcerated sores, and the gum, though apparently *poisonous*, was chewed (but *never swallowed*) as a kind of chewing gum and as a cure for bad breath.

They collected the gum by making cuts in the bark and used it also to scent hair oil and ointments by heating it until it dissolved in the seed oil or pigeon-fat base.

Rangiora's flowering also signalled the fourth Māori month (September) – time for planting the kūmara crop.

Its striking leaves make it a good specimen tree. Can also be planted as part of a shrub border and pruned if necessary. Somewhat frost tender (especially when young) but will tolerate wind. Grows easily from cuttings.

Taraire

Beilschmiedia tarairi

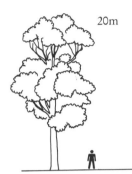

20m

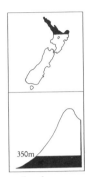

350m

Leaves: dark green above, leathery, usually whitish beneath, mostly 7–14cm long

Fruit: in autumn, 3.5cm long, dark purple

Other: buds, new branches and leaf veins all covered in *fine brown hair*

Nature Notes: fruit are enjoyed by wood pigeon, that is, if possums have not got to them first. Bees collect nectar and pollen from the inconspicuous flowers in spring.

Uses: The kernel of the largish, purple-black taraire fruit was one of the staple foods of forest-dwelling Māori. The thin flesh surrounding it, though sweet enough to be occasionally eaten by children, often tastes too strongly of turpentine to be of much use. Traditionally the kernels were first steamed for a couple of days in a hāngi but they can also be boiled for an hour or roasted in the embers of a campfire. The texture is like a slimy version of a potato, though the sliminess is greatly reduced by roasting.

The heartwood will last untreated for interior use but untreated sapwood is subject to borer attack. An easy timber to saw, machine and turn, taking a good finish, taraire is well suited to furniture making. This was one of its 19th century uses, along with the manufacture of ships' blocks and light carts. The wood has also occasionally been used for interior finishing of houses and with preservative treatment for subfloor framing. Though sometimes offered for sale as firewood, it tends to burn too quickly.

Recommended as a shapely specimen tree with fine, bold foliage, grown successfully as far south as Christchurch when protected from frost. Generally grown from seed. Does best in a rich, well-drained soil, in a slightly sheltered and shady position. Quick to germinate, relatively quick growing and ideal for attracting birds.

Kauri

Agathis australis

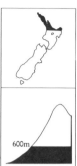

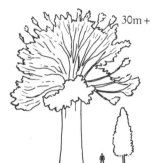

30m +

600m

Leaves: alternating to almost opposite, mostly 2–4cm long (longer on young trees)

Cones: in spring and summer, female cones round, male finger-shaped

Trunk: hammer marked, mostly grey, falling in large thick flakes

Other: bleeding gum common on or under tree

Nature Notes: the forks of mature kauri support over 50 kinds of shrubs and tuft plants, such as the flax-like kahakaha.

Uses: Taking impressions for making dentures might seem an odd use for a tree, but kauri gum was once an ingredient of a compound used for just that. But the gum's main commercial and export uses involved dissolving the fresh, milky gum or clear, sub-fossilised resin in linseed oil for making varnish and as a raw material for manufacturing paint and linoleum.

The dust or scrapings of this gum were used as a fire kindler or torch fuel. Māori burnt the old gum to produce a tattooing pigment and used the fresh gum for chewing. They also burnt it to kill or deter pest insects in kūmara plantations. The harder, more transparent kind was even turned into mouthpieces for smokers' pipes.

Kauri was said to be the most versatile native timber. Apart from the usual range of house, ship and cart building uses, it was favoured for church pews and post office counters. Northern Māori have prized it for large carvings and canoes. Nowadays, demolition kauri, stumps and fallen trees remain popular with the woodturner.

While still in its young, conical shape – a shape it retains for 50 years at least – kauri makes an attractive specimen tree. Easy to grow from fresh seed – pick the round, female cones when mature (in March) and leave them in the sun until they ripen and fall apart to release the small winged seeds. Sow these within three weeks. Quick to germinate.

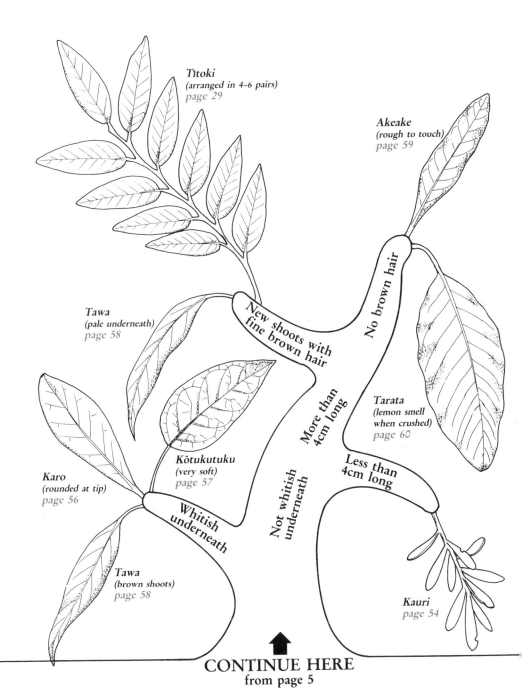

Tītoki
(arranged in 4–6 pairs)
page 29

Akeake
(rough to touch)
page 59

Tawa
(pale underneath)
page 58

New shoots with
fine brown hair

No brown hair

Kōtukutuku
(very soft)
page 57

More than
4cm long

Tarata
*(lemon smell
when crushed)*
page 60

Karo
(rounded at tip)
page 56

Whitish
underneath

Not whitish
underneath

Less than
4cm long

Tawa
(brown shoots)
page 58

Kauri
page 54

CONTINUE HERE
from page 5

55

Karo

Pittosporum crassifolium

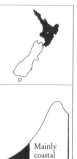

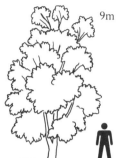

Mainly coastal

9m

Leaves: *alternating* (unlike pōhutukawa), *whitish beneath*, 4–7cm long

Flowers: mainly in early spring, red to purple, about 1cm across, heavily scented (especially in evening)

Fruit: in autumn, round and green, about 2cm across, bursting to reveal sticky black seeds

Nature Notes: bees collect nectar from the flowers in spring. Nectar and seeds attract birds.

Uses: Although greatly valued as an ornamental and shelter tree, karo appears to have had no specific Māori usage. It does not even rank as a good firewood and the white timber, though very tough, has been used mostly in marquetry or inlaying.

To the horticulturist though, karo not only has the virtue of being easy to grow, but is also both versatile and attractive. Its extreme resistance to even the strongest salt winds makes it an ideal shelter tree especially in coastal situations. From as far back as the late 19th century it has been recommended for helping to stabilise inland sand dunes. Its ability to withstand trimming makes it popular too for hedges both here and as far afield as Cornwall, England.

The flowers produce a rich scent, particularly noticeable on still evenings in early spring, and provide a worthwhile source of nectar for bees and some birds. Birds also are attracted to karo's sticky seeds which appear when the three- or four-part capsules split, thus providing the tree with an effective means of seed dispersal.

Germinates easily from fallen seed and transplants well. Growing from cuttings is more difficult. Several varieties have been developed including at least one variegated form.

Kōtukutuku
Tree Fuchsia
Fuchsia excorticata

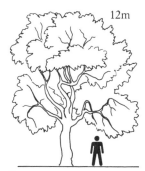

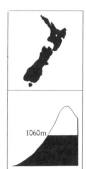

Leaves: few or no teeth, *white beneath* with furry veins, soft. In the south, loses its leaves in winter

Flowers: in late spring, hanging, dark purple

Fruit: in summer, dark purple to almost black, narrow and about 1cm long

Trunk: *loose papery bark*

Nature Notes: bellbird, silvereye and tui eat the nectar. Wood pigeon, tui, white-head and possums feed on fruit. Bees collect pollen and nectar.

Uses: Known in some areas as kōnini, but strictly speaking this is the name of the sweet, edible fruit. The fruit were eaten by early Māori and many Pākehā enjoyed them too – either raw, as an ingredient in jams, stewed with honey or in the form of a pudding. One source, with a more literary bent, tells us that kōnini berries make a good ink.

Homespinners use the bark or decayed wood to produce a range of colours from straw and yellow ochre through green-gold and pinkish-maize to purple, brown and black.

For Māori, kōtukutuku blossoms, in some areas at least, also signalled the time for planting kūmara, in the fourth month of their calendar (September). The tree had medicinal use as one ingredient in vapour baths used by Māori women after childbirth.

Though one of the strongest and most durable native timbers, the gnarled and curved nature of the trunks saved it from large-scale exploitation. Not much used these days, it was once prized for a variety of ornamental uses including woodturning. It is almost impossible to burn and hence is one of the trees to earn the bushman's nickname 'bucket of water wood'.

Occasionally grown for its gnarled appearance and papery bark. Grows very easily from seed or cuttings.

Tawa
Beilschmiedia tawa

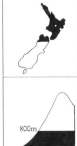

24m+

800m

Leaves: 6–10cm long, alternating to almost opposite, *pale to white beneath*; hanging, graceful and willow-like, *brown fur* on new growth

Fruit: in late summer, dark purple to black, 2–3cm long

Trunk: dark, smooth. Older trees often buttressed at base

Nature Notes: fruit popular with wood pigeon and kākā. The tiny, green flowers supply pollen and nectar to bees in spring. Large, blue-black and gold tawa longhorn beetles (25mm long) sometimes found on broken branches.

Uses: When perfectly ripe, the purple-black flesh of the fruit has a sweetish, slightly turpentine flavour, but it was the cooked kernels which were most prized by early Māori as food – sometimes dried and stored for years as a standby. They were usually steamed in a hāngi for two days, but also occasionally boiled or roasted in embers. They taste similar to potato but slimy in texture. Roasting is better.

The bark was used medicinally for stomach pain and colds; 19th century trampers infused the bark to make a sweet tea. Early Māori fashioned the wood into long shafts for bird spears and made battens for the roofs and walls of whare.

Tawa's ripe berries will dye wool purple or green depending on the mordant used. Large-scale use of the timber began in the 1800s with coopers making dairy buckets and tubs, casks and butter kegs. It has since been widely used for woodturning, clothes pegs, furniture and flooring, papermaking and firewood. It is a shameful reflection on our nation's values that natural tawa forests are still being felled for wood pulp rather than trees being planted for the purpose.

Delicate, drooping leaves give it a graceful appearance, making it a fine specimen tree. Good for attracting birds. Grows easily from seed. Quick to germinate.

Akeake

Dodonaea viscosa

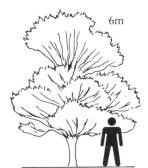

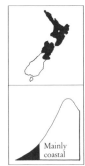

Leaves: *sandpapery to touch* (unlike tawa), no teeth, 4–7cm long, sometimes reddish

Seeds: in summer (female trees only), seed capsules 1.5cm across with 2–3 wings

Trunk: flaking reddish bark

Other: young shoots can be slightly sticky

Nature Notes: honey bees collect pollen and nectar from the inconspicuous flowers between September and January.

Uses: Akeake timber is one of the hardest native woods, so hard that a falling axe can literally bounce off it. Its remarkable density made it particularly useful to Māori for making clubs and other weapons. More recent settlers put it to similar use when making heads for mauls used in bushfelling. And when brass was in short supply, it even proved effective in making machine bearings. Cabinetmakers have valued it for inlaid work and picture frames; sculptors claim it equal to the more traditional box wood for making modelling tools.

The twigs have been used to produce a number of dyes: pale green, yellow-green, beige grey and bright gold.

Although Māori reputedly used the leaves (or more likely the lemon-eucalyptus smelling seeds) to make a kind of perfume, they do not seem to have used the tree medicinally. Surprising, since the same tree has found medicinal use in Indonesia, Reunion Island, Kanaky (New Caledonia), Tahiti, Hawaii, Australia, Panama and Peru – for quite a variety of ailments but most commonly for reducing fevers.

A useful hedge or shelter tree in exposed or coastal areas. The unusual seed capsules are used in flower arranging. Grows easily from seed (collected before the winged capsules open). Purplish-red and cream-edged leaved varieties are available.

Tarata
Lemonwood
Pittosporum eugenioides

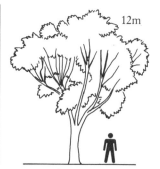

12m

600m

Leaves: *lemon-scented when crushed* (unlike tawa), very glossy on top, edges wavy, midvein and leaf stalk pale cream, *7–15cm long* (unlike kōhūhū)

Flowers: in late spring, starry, cream, in bunches, sweet smelling

Other: grows alongside streams and in open forest

Nature Notes: bees collect pollen and nectar. A parasitic native mistletoe (tāpia) is sometimes found on trees north of Auckland. Large, patterned blisters sometimes seen beneath the leaves are made by the sixpenny scale insect.

Uses: Anyone who has ever smelled the delightful lemon-carrot scent of the crushed leaf or the sweet fragrance of the flowers, will not be surprised to learn that early Māori used tarata for perfume. The flowers, or crushed leaves, were mixed with fat to make a body lotion, and the gum bled from vertical grooves cut in the trunk was added to oil from the crushed seeds of tītoki or the native vine, kōhia (New Zealand passion-flower) to make a scented body oil.

The same resinous gum was chewed to cure bad breath or made into chewing gum by mixing it with the bitter, dried sap of pūhā. When chewed into a paste, the leaves reportedly make an effective lotion for saddle sores on horses.

The timber is strong, tough and elastic, once favoured for the handles of carpenters' tools and woodturning generally. It makes poor firewood.

Not surprisingly, it was one of the first plants sent to the Royal Botanic Gardens at Kew in England and by 1872 it had already become a favourite in ornamental green-houses in southern France. A shapely specimen tree, appreciated for its glossy, wavy-edged leaves and showy scented flowers. Makes a good hedge or lower tier in a farm shelter belt. Grows easily and quickly from fully ripened seed.

Conspicuous Flowers and Berries

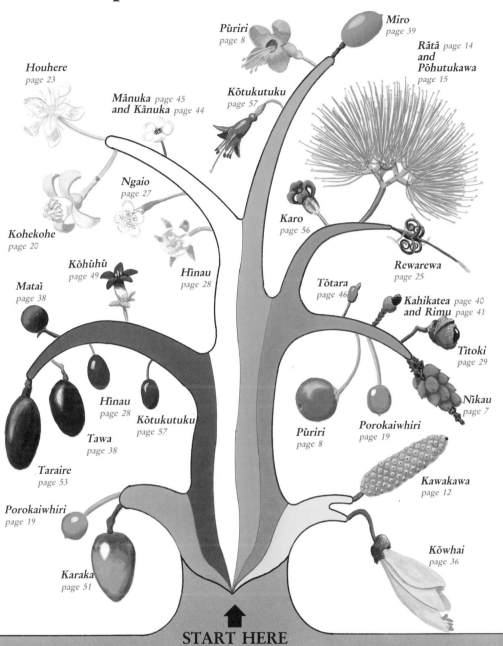

Pūriri
page 8

Miro
page 39

Rātā page 14
and
Pōhutukawa
page 15

Houhere
page 23

Mānuka page 45
and Kānuka page 44

Kōtukutuku
page 57

Ngaio
page 27

Karo
page 56

Kohekohe
page 20

Kōhūhū
page 49

Hīnau
page 28

Rewarewa
page 25

Matai
page 38

Tōtara
page 46

Kahikatea page 40
and Rimu page 41

Titoki
page 29

Hīnau
page 28

Kōtukutuku
page 57

Tawa
page 38

Pūriri
page 8

Porokaiwhiri
page 19

Nīkau
page 7

Taraire
page 53

Kawakawa
page 12

Porokaiwhiri
page 19

Karaka
page 51

Kōwhai
page 36

START HERE

Troubleshooting

If the tree has a very tall, branchless trunk (so that the leaves are way out of reach), then check: does it take two or more adults to hug the tree? If no, go to ✻ If yes, then look at the bark:

Does it fall in circular flakes like this?

OR

Peel off in long papery strips, like this?

OR

Have other kinds of flakes, like this?

Most likely it is a kauri (p. 54), mataī (p. 38) or miro (p. 39)

Most likely it is a tōtara (p. 46)

Most likely it is a rimu (p. 41), kahikatea (p. 40) or rātā (p. 14)

Now, to find out which of these trees it is,
✻ look on the ground for fallen leaves and use the leaf key (p. 5).

If you have trouble matching your leaf with the key:

1 Are you sure the leaf is from a **tree?** Shrubs (which are generally smaller than trees and have no central trunk) are not covered.

2 Are you sure it is a **native?** If found in native forest, it most probably is native. Found elsewhere, it may not be.

3 Are you sure it is a **typical adult** leaf? Leaves often vary a lot, especially between seedling and adult trees.

4 Are you sure the tree is a **common** one? Others are not covered.

5 Is it a **tree fern?** Tree ferns are not covered. But in case it helps: there are eight kinds found on the main islands, the commonest being ponga (the one with silver undersides to its fronds) and mamaku (the one with very thick, black frond stems).

If the key is still not working, then take a closer look at the leaf:

1 Are you sure about whether it has teeth along the edges? The teeth on ngaio and hīnau leaves, for example, are easy to miss.

2 Are you sure about whether the leaves are opposite or alternate? Taraire and kauri leaves may at first glance appear to be all opposite.

3 Did you remember to start at the *bottom* of the first leaf key (p. 5)?

Selected References

Aston, B.C. The Indigenous Tans and Vegetable Dyestuffs of New Zealand. Parts I & II. *NZJ Agriculture* 15: 55–62, 1917; 15: 117–28, 1917 & 16: 358–65, 1918.

Beever, James. *A Dictionary of Maori Plant Names.* Auckland Botanical Society, 1987.

Best, Elsdon. *Forest Lore of the Maori.* Government Printer, 1977.

Best, Elsdon. *The Maori Division of Time.* Government Printer, 1986.

Brooker, S.G., Cambie, R.C. and Cooper, R.C. *Economic Native Plants of New Zealand.* Botany Division, DSIR, 1988.

Brooker, S.G., Cambie, R.C. and Cooper, R.C. *New Zealand Medicinal Plants.* Heinemann, 1987.

Connor, H.E. *The Poisonous Plants in New Zealand.* Government Printer, 1977.

Crowe, Andrew. *Native Edible Plants of New Zealand.* Hodder & Stoughton, 1990.

Fisher, Muriel and Power, Elaine. *A Touch of Nature.* Collins, 1980.

Hutchinson, Amy. *Plant Dyeing.* The Daily Telegraph Co., Napier, 1941.

Kirk, T. *The Forest Flora of New Zealand.* Government Printer, 1889.

Laing, R.M. and Blackwell, E.W. *Plants of New Zealand.* Whitcombe & Tombs, 1964.

Lloyd, Joyce. *Dyes from Plants of Australia and New Zealand.* Reed, 1981.

Massey, Brian. *Woodturning in New Zealand.* Government Printer, 1987.

McDermott, Mike. *Woodturning with New Zealand Timbers.* Reed Methuen, 1985.

Metcalf, L.J. *The Cultivation of New Zealand Trees and Shrubs.* Reed Methuen, 1987.

Milner, Ann. *Natural Wool Dyes and Recipes.* John McIndoe, 1979.

Moore, L.B. & Irwin, J.B. *The Oxford Book of New Zealand Plants.* Oxford University Press, 1978.

Mortimer, John & Bunny. *Trees for the New Zealand Countryside.* Butterworths, 1987.

Pendergrast, Mick. *Feathers and Fibre.* Penguin, 1984.

Reid, J.S. *New Zealand Building Timbers.* New Zealand Forest Service, 1956.

Richards, E.C. *Our New Zealand Trees and Flowers.* Simpson & Williams, 1956.

Taylor, Rev. Richard. Vegetable Productions of New Zealand. *New Zealand Journal,* p.68–69, 25 March 1848.

Taylor, Rev. Richard. *A Leaf from the Natural History of New Zealand.* Chapman, 1870.

Walsh, R.S. *Nectar and Pollen Sources of New Zealand.* National Beekeepers' Association of New Zealand, 1978.

Index